A Bride's Guide to an Elegant Wedding with a Low Budget

I0424865

By Meloni Ann Huddleston

Copyright 2012

ISBN   978-1-257-81776-4

Contents

I'd like to dedicate this guide to my wonderful mother, Pastor Litha V. Ford of the Center of JoY Christian Ministries of Saint Louis, Missouri.

Mother, God has blessed you in a package. You've got the whole package; the love, the passion, the grace and the intelligence to never separate the love of God from all the activities of your daily life. You manage to live within the blessings God has bestowed upon you and sharing them with your children, your grandchildren and your great grandchildren. I personally thank you for guiding me to the right, toward heaven. You have given me strength to do all the things I long to do. I thank you for your motherly love and support even when I wasn't obedient. You are the sunshine of my life and I love you,

Meloni

Introduction

I once owned a wedding chapel to offer people who wanted to get married an elegant atmosphere that didn't cost thousands of dollars. It was a small quaint, cozy and warm chapel I would have chosen to use before I chose to vow to be married in the courthouse.

I realized that weddings really do own character but the character wasn't measured by how much money was spent on the wedding. Elegance is character and I discovered that not everyone knew how to grasp it. It seemed you either had it within or you didn't. But, I was there to help and I enjoyed every single minute of it.

I've decided to share a few tips and secrets on how to simply have an elegant ceremony without spending thousands of dollars. As you read, open your imagination. Imagine yourself and imagine what is best for you.

Meaning of a Low Budgets

The definition of a low budget is relative. However, regardless of how much money you have or don't have, you can still have an elegant and beautiful wedding. You can take advantage of this book regardless of what amount of money you're planning to spend.

I've been to a countless number of weddings. I've coordinated a few. I am a wedding fanatic. I love weddings. I love to see people in love and make an ultimate commitment.

So, with the help of this guide, you can actually have hardly any money and plan to have an elegant wedding.

The heart of elegancy is vision and mood. Unfortunately, not all of us are equipped with discerning either. I was blessed to create both without using a lot of money. In a lot of instances "less is more"; but money sure wouldn't apply to that, now would it?

Less is more while planning weddings and other celebrations. It doesn't take a whole lot of money or anything else when we can keep the reason for the celebration at the forefront.

A low budget wedding at the end of the day would have created the same impact as a wedding that used a budget of tens of thousands of dollars. All you want is to be pleased but for most brides, they would want their guests to be pleased and utter the words, "That was beautiful". Well, most of us guests do because it was beautiful. All weddings are.

So, I'm here to save you a few bucks. You will see me write, "Think smart" and "less is more" repetitiously. Thinking smart is the key in this economy nowadays. We can get a big bang from small gun if we know how and if we are willing to sacrifice.

Planning

This is the huge part of setting the mood of elegance for your wedding. Planning a wedding regardless of the theme, where it is to be held, the venue of the reception, and the honeymoon, should take over a few days or even weeks. That depends on what you're doing. Have you ever completed something and say to yourself, "Oh, I should have..."? Well, you can alleviate those type of thoughts when you plan over a period of time.

Take the time to write down what you are able to do with the budget you've set. Write it all down. Leave it for a couple of days and I guarantee you, you will go back and make changes. After you make the changes, go back. Continue to do this until you've clinched or I like to use "mainstreamed" your idea for your wedding.

While you are planning, let me give you a few tips. Here are points where you can actually cut cost – way down.

- Your gown and appearance doesn't have to be greatly expensive
- The groom's attire doesn't have to be traditional as long as it looks good on him
- The ceremony does not have to cost thousands of dollars
- The reception and honeymoon can be modified

You can compromise between those five parts of your wedding. Do not be afraid to do what suits your budget and to do what is best for you and your marriage.

Your gown and appearance: Choose a gown or dress (hello) that looks good on you! Accessorize it with some sparkle and bling. Find shoes that look good on you. These things are all that matter. If it looks good and you've chosen in good taste, it will be elegant. Remember less is more.

Treat your hair as you normally do. Find some pictures online and try to duplicate it yourself; if you can't, find a friend who will do it for no cost.

Buns and balls are usually always elegant and if you're going to go that route, guess what, you can make your own veil! Google it or find it on the Youtube! If you decide not to wear a veil, you can wrap your ball with pearls or rhinestones. Staggered pearl pins, or rhinestone pins creates an elegant look as well. Keep it simple and not botchy. Don't overdo it.

In reality, a bride can feel pretty and elegant with hardly anything to do to herself.

The groom's attire: Changing a tie with a suit will suffice for some wedding themes. If the groom is determined to wear a tux, that's fine. Usually tux rentals aren't that costly, but remember this may be for a special day but it still only lasts a few hours. Be smart.

There's more about tuxedos later in the guide. Have in mind that grooms and groomsmen usually do what they are told. I'm not sure if they really care as much as the bride and bridesmaids. This is a good thing.

The ceremony: What is it really that makes the ceremony, "beautiful"? The flowers and candles are nice. All the decorations are beautiful, right? But beauty is in the tone of the vow exchange. The quietness of the witnesses while the vows are being spoken aloud and the altar appeal are the biggest details you should be more concerned about. Money should be allotted for the altar décor and the aisle and sideshow décor can be determined by the size of the budget.

Here is a really good tip. If you are going to have a rehearsal, is there a need for a coordinator? You may feel better having one but ceremony coordinators are useful with weddings that have children in them for flowers and ring pillows. You still can have that. At the rehearsal, pick someone to get the children down the aisle at their appropriate times. All adults should be able to handle going down the aisle when they're suppose to go down. This can be stressed at the rehearsal. In other words, you can be the coordinator at the rehearsal to save yourself a few bucks. Trust me it will be fine. Less than perfect weddings are beautiful too. Weddings aren't perfect anyway; that's something all in the bride's head. If you just want or need a coordinator without being too involved,

tell a friend what you want and have a friend to do it for you. Paying for a coordinator can be omitted for a low budget wedding without compromising the elegance of the wedding.

The reception and honeymoon: Are you planning to have a reception? An allotment for a wedding reception venue, for most weddings, big and small is usually the bulk of the budget. The only way to get around it is to not have a reception until you have enough funds to spare. Be smart again here. We all wanted to show off or be seen but at what cost? You can find venues for a small group as low as thirty. If you have a great number of guests with little money, you may need to get some help or consider not having a reception; and the same goes with a honeymoon.

The reception and honeymoon will eat up your entire budget! Allot according to what is important to you, but remember if the wedding itself is more important to you, you can do it with little money.

This is the time to make the decisions. You don't have to stick to them but you should have a solid idea which direction you're going and try to stay on course.

Many people start with a budget of five to ten thousand dollars and end up over budget with credit card debt that may take years to pay off. Always consider the future when you are making your plans. You may want to have the best and prettiest wedding of them all but do you want to start a marriage in debt?

To me, it's perfectly fine to want to get married for whatever reason and do so without having the pressures of spending money on a wedding reception and a honeymoon. You can plan on dinner afterwards for close family. Then you can have plans to spend a few nights in one of the fine hotels in your local city.

You can spend hardly anything to get married and save the rest for the celebration reception and honeymoon or you can lavishly spend for your ceremony (for the pictures) and skip the

celebration and honeymoon, or yet take a honeymoon after a small private vow exchange in front of a elegantly made altar you can put just about anywhere.

I'm a very creative person with an enormous imagination. There are lots of ways to reflect your personality in your wedding without spending lots of money.

You may need to search for good deals on invitations. I find the elegant, prettier ones aren't cheap. So allot for invitations if you are going to use invitations. Some invitations can be hand-made if you know a calligrapher. Invitations are the only gray area I have with budgets for weddings. That is because if you are going to present yourself before witnesses then that means they were invited. Invitations are the first impression you present to your guests. It gives them the idea of what kind of wedding you are planning. I think a pretty invitation with personality is warranted. Allot your budget for invitations for sure. It may not be costly if you are only ordering twenty-five or thirty.

Low Budget Wedding Ideas

The first idea I'm going to present to you is not an uncommon one. People have chosen to use their own home for their wedding ceremony since the beginning of time. Depending on how big or small your home is will determine how many guests to invite. Most times when a home is used, close family and friends are the only invited guests.

Look at the space and determine where would be the best place for the altar and where would be the best place for your guests to stand and witness. Those are the two important concerns.

After you have determined where the altar is going to be created, make a list of the materials you want to include for your altar. The list could include:

- Tulle
- Pedestal (s)
- Candles
- Flowers

Of course "tulle" is the cloth of choice for draping. You can either buy or rent a white pedestal or two. They are decently priced in many places. Choose which flowers you want to use. Choose carefully. You do not want to use flowers normally seen at funerals. You can use real flowers (best but more expensive) or you can use silk flowers which can be expensive as well but if you catch a craft store with a sale, you will find savings using silk flowers. Silk flowers look better to me. Remember this is a one day use of all these things. Do not get so caught up in making things perfect. It will be perfect because mentally you are staging your own perfection with what YOU want to use at YOUR altar. The pictures will be beautiful.

Allow your guest to mingle a little before the ceremony. You can make a presence from a room with a door, a staircase, the outside (back or front door). Look and assess what you have to work with.

While your guests are mingling, your photographer, or whomever you've chosen to take pictures can video your guest congratulating the two of you. It makes a great keepsake and you can enjoy for years to come.

The second idea is the use of a public park with a gazebo preferably. Wedding pictures with gazebos, grass and trees are simply beautiful. The only snag about using the outdoors is being able to count on the weather. If it doesn't rain, you may be alright. Light winds are beautiful but strong winds can be horrifying. So think smart before choosing to use the outdoor idea or have a backup plan in case of in climate weather.

Gazebos are easy to decorate for your altar; just drape the rails with tulle and flowers. I've seen people dressed in the same color as the drapes but a different color than the wedding party to be used as candle holders; one for his, one for hers and the unity candle. In case of winds, they could keep a fire with their hands. It was actually quite neat.

Your guests can either stand or sit depending on your budget. If there's no tent venue for a reception in the same area, I suggest they stand until the reception, if a reception is planned.

Be creative in the park. Use all the beautiful scenery the park has to offer for your pictures.

The third idea is one that I've used myself. I can tell you a lot about it. It was my second marriage and my fiancée and I did not want to spend bunches of money.

This is where you will spend a lot of time on the internet. Research and look into all the little chapels in Las Vegas, Nevada that you can before you make your choice. There are some good ones and probably some that aren't so good. I was only interested in the chapels that offered pictures and videos; preferably 360 degree virtual tours. I say this because if you book your date you have to pay and if you can't see all of it before you book and pay, you may get there and change your mind or maybe put yourself in a frenzy trying to find another chapel with an opening date and time that you are there.

It was quite fun looking at the many chapels Las Vegas had to offer. I noticed a chapel who offered a price list for my budget. I loved the idea. The same chapel offered videos of ceremonies within the last two weeks; so enjoyed looking at a few before I decided that chapel would be the one.

There are so many chapels in Las Vegas and I am positive I didn't get through half before I made a decision. My thoughts are synced with the purpose of writing this guide and sharing them with you. A true marriage will be determined after the vows are taken. I thought it would be wise for me to spend less time and energy trying to create a perfect wedding and instead direct that force to the sustainability of my marriage. In other words, it was past time for me to be married. I had been dating for years.

I wanted beautiful pictures and most of my money kept in my bank accounts.

Mon Bel Ami, French for "my beautiful friend", was the name of the chapel. I don't mind plugging them because they were very nice and very helpful. We purchased the small package, but we had to tip the coordinator, tip the officiator, and tip the photographer; about sixty dollars each. The salesperson will try to sell you a few of the pictures but the idea is to sell all the pictures so plan to buy all the pictures and they will usually give you a good deal. This is probably the routine at all the chapels in Vegas, so be prepared.

You can obtain your marriage license in Las Vegas and get married right outside the building after you get it. There was no waiting period. We waited in line about ten minutes before we used our driver's licenses and birth certificates to get the marriage license.

You can wear what you like. You can create your own mood or theme. The Elvis theme costs a little more, I wasn't interested. I wore a wedding gown I purchased there in Vegas for one hundred dollars and my groom packed a tux he normally kept in his closet, but a black suit would have sufficed and a cream, ivory or champagne colored dress would have sufficed as well.

Plan your day in Vegas. It's pretty easy being in Vegas. You could see a show after dinner or play games in your wedding gown or all three.

We used our time share for lodging and our frequent flyer points for our flights. We attended three timeshare presentations to get free dinner and a free show. Needless to say, we didn't spend much to get married but we have pictures that look as if we spent a million dollars. It was an unforgettable experience.

I invited my son and his friend because they had never been and picked up the tab after they got there but didn't spend much.

If family and friends are invited to join you in Vegas, let them know ahead of time the need for them to pay for their expenses, if that is the case.

The last idea I have to offer is one of the most simple and personal ways of getting married. I've seen pictures of military weddings and it seems there were maybe three other people in an office room; no flowers, no candles, no tulle, nothing, although I believe there were officers present. I thought it was personal and simple but elegant in spirit.

For those who want to get married without all the hoopla, this idea may interest you. Military weddings seem to be elegant automatically. If you have this opportunity, do not hesitate.

In General:

The word, "small" means two to ten important people, the officiate and the persons that are close to you, your witnesses.

Wherever the officiate stands is the altar.

You may decide to hold a flower but most times in this instance, the bride and groom are usually holding hands. This is a very intimate setting where the bride and groom are eager for whatever reason to be married. Their surroundings don't really matter because the tones of their hearts are already set to be married.

This idea is definitely used for the mature bride and groom who have already experienced the wedding setting with flowers and decorations.

These couples may opt to skip a formal reception as well. Usually a formal dinner party with a few family members and friends is scheduled, but it doesn't have to be.

We don't have to be ashamed of how we choose to get married. What's shameful is how we spend thousands of dollars on weddings and the marriage only lasts a few months to a couple of years.

These statements aren't directed to people who have money to spend lavishly on weddings and choose to do so regardless of how long the marriage last. I want to enlighten the less fortunate in these hard economical times by assuring them that the elegance in weddings doesn't directly correlate with the amount of money of spent on them.

The Gown, the Tux, the Rings

Your wedding gown or dress will be memorable. While you're choosing or shopping for a gown, take into consideration the slew of things. The gown does not have to be the most expensive item on your budget. It should fit you comfortably and you should feel good in it. You can accessorize the simple gown if you like.

Do not over accessorize a fancy hairdo. Keep it simple and uncomplicated. Remember less is more. Keep close to your budget.

The tuxedo can be found on sale in several stores. If not, check out the rental fee for it. Know ahead of time if a tuxedo is something the groom needs to keep in his closet for future use if you're thinking about buying it. Remember weddings are only for a few hours and yet while we want to create fond memories, we don't want to go over budget. For starters, we need to ask the groom if he is interested in wearing a tuxedo. Some grooms are particular about comfort. They want to be comfortable at all times and wearing a tuxedo may not make him comfortable. If it doesn't, that eliminates the tux cost; move on to a different look. Grooms can wear a black suit with matching color tie to create and elegant look to the wedding.

Rings in my book are never to be compromised. You don't have to spend thousands of dollars on rings but the bride and groom should exchange the type of ring in which both will wear daily. I've seen everything with ring exchange from strings and tattoos to the million dollar gem.

You can get a bargain at your local pawn shop, I'm sure. If that doesn't please you and your budget is tight, I would stick with simple bands for starters. Wedding bands are simple but they are being created nowadays with a little flare for both the bride and groom.

Maybe later you could add a diamond ring on an anniversary or Christmas.

While it is important to exchange bands, it is also important to understand why it is done therefore why married people really should wear their rings. It (the exchange) symbolizes love and marriage. It connects two souls even when they're not connected or when they are apart.

Some of us believe that a piece of jewelry doesn't solidify who we are so we immediately omit buying rings or we may cease wearing them. I plead you not to do that. If the costs for rings are in your budget, buy them and wear them.

The Rehearsal

Cut cost here. Why do you need a formal rehearsal? You can have a rehearsal but it does not have to include all the traditional amenities for others. If you can't rehearse where you're going to wed, choose a spot for those that are in the wedding and go over "what's next" with everyone. A friend or family member can do this for you.

Ceremonies are elegant when whatever is next, is done without question or pause. Order creates mood. Mood creates elegance. All you need to do is select someone to make sure the next thing in order gets done without being noticed.

Rehearsal is where everything is solidified. After rehearsal everyone involved should feel good about their role in the wedding. Emotions of peace and understanding create elegance. You'll see more smiles and less nervousness. If the wedding is small it will probably be dainty and easier to handle without the stress.

Reception Venues and Ideas

Skip it if you don't have enough funds. I know that's hard to do but you can plan a reception later. If you're like me you want everyone to see you dance with your husband and you may want to show off a bit, right? Here is what you do. Allot for the reception first. Whatever you have left over, you may have to compromise tremendously to make this work. It can work.

Find a venue that you can afford. Do not try to show off by going over your head subsequently over your budget.

I'd rather skip the reception if I had to let family or friends cater it. That usually turns out to be a "potluck" type of reception. Those aren't elegant. They work but it's not anything different than what we are already used to doing. Someone got married in this instance so let's just remember not to go too far in desperate times. Let us not ruin what was elegant an hour ago to a desperate event.

Check your funds. How many people can you afford to feed? What kind of food? Where will this take place? Will there be music and dancing? How much is the cake? Do I need to hire a DJ or band? Consider all these things and narrow down to what's important to you at this time.

It may be that your budget will only allow for you to feed ten to twenty people. Choose them and create a venue at a nice restaurant. Be creative with the reception but do not sacrifice elegance to pleasure others.

Remember you can always hop into whatever transportation you've selected to go directly to the airport after the ceremony. How fun does that sound? You could eliminate the reception and coordinate your times for ending the ceremony and departure to somewhere like Sedona, Arizona or San Francisco, California. I'm inspiring you to be creative.

Honeymooning on a Low Budget

Consummations are important but let us analyze the circumstances seriously before we go all out for the honeymoon.

Consider the number of times you've been married. Consider your living arrangements before the ceremony. Consider quality and quantity of your past sexual encounters.

In a no sexual contact before marriage situation we should allot a little more for a honeymoon. This is an exciting time! Why not be in an exciting place? The newness of intimacy demands its rightful environment.

Some of the less expensive places to visit are places in the USA (if your are already in the USA) are places like Las Vegas, Orlando, or maybe some of the mountainous areas in Georgia or Pennsylvania. There are several lovely places to visit in the USA they may be a little bit more expensive but maybe less expensive than leaving the country. If you have funds to leave the country, some of the less expensive areas for a honeymoon are Mexico and Canada. There are several beautiful beaches in Mexico and Vancouver, Montreal, Quebec, Victoria, and Whistler in Canada.

This is an area you will need to spend time. If you want to cut cost start looking early and if you want to have a really good time, research the area you've decided to visit. Maybe someone you know has been there and you can ask about the things to do there. If not, AAA Vacation Club can help you.

Here are ideas for the folk interested in spending hardly any money at all, for whatever reason.

It is always exciting being somewhere new with the one you truly love, your wife or your husband. Though the intimacy is not new, it can be renewed with a honeymoon.

A trip to the finest hotel in your residing city could be hopeful and fun. A road trip to the closest biggest city could be fun as well. Or, you could fly to the closest city and stay the weekend at a bed and breakfast.

A weekday or two in a historical city would be nice with a tour guide to educate yourself about the city. Anything different in this case may be promising for the couples who are already sexually active.

Of course you should take each other's interest into consideration before selecting.

If the plan is to do nothing but enjoy each other's company, that's an idea where less money is needed. It's conducive to your low budget.

You don't have to spend money to enjoy the company of your spouse. That is free.

Summary

There is a terrific span of character for weddings. I've seen some really lovely ones and I've seen some really bad ones.

When brides find themselves frustrated and stressed, that is the point where she needs to take over and probably downsize the whole idea. There isn't a wedding I can't forget. Most of us forget them all. However, we never forget the words that were spoken or the tears that fell. We never forget the song that was sung or the beautiful melody of it. But I promise you whatever it is that the bride is stressing over, we've forgotten.

Create your budget and stick to it. By doing this you will have given your marriage a healthy start, not so common in our lifestyles today.

May the Lord bless you and keep you. I wish you well and all that is comforting during the planning of your wedding, your wedding but most of all, your marriage.

www.ingramcontent.com/pod-product-compliance
Lightning Source LLC
Chambersburg PA
CBHW061232280526
45784CB00006B/2737